Be Brave, little one.
I love you!
♡ -Aunt Catherine

A Child's First Book of
TRUMP

Michael Ian Black   Marc Rosenthal

Simon & Schuster BFYR

New York London Toronto Sydney New Delhi

Simon & Schuster BFYR • An imprint of Simon & Schuster Children's Publishing Division • 1230 Avenue of the Americas, New York, New York 10020 • Text copyright © 2016 by Hot Schwartz Productions • Illustrations copyright © 2016 by Marc Rosenthal • All rights reserved, including the right of reproduction in whole or in part in any form. • Simon & Schuster BFYR is a trademark of Simon & Schuster, Inc. • For information about special discounts for bulk purchases, please contact Simon & Schuster Special Sales at 1-866-506-1949 or business@ simonandschuster.com. • Simon & Schuster to your Speakers Bureau can bring authors live event. For more information or to book an event, contact the Simon & Schuster Speakers Bureau at 1-866-248-3049 or visit our website at www.simonspeakers.com. • Book design by Dan Potash • The text for this book was set in Goudy Sans. • The illustrations for this book were drawn in pencil and colored digitally. • Manufactured in the United States of America • 0616 PCH • First Edition • 2 4 6 8 10 9 7 5 3 1 CIP data for this book is available from the Library of Congress. • ISBN 978-1-4814-8800-6 • ISBN 978-1-4814-8801-3 (eBook)

For the haters and losers—M. I. B.

To Will and Julia. May their futures be bright and Trumpless—M. R.

*D*ear reader, I know that you might be confused

After spotting this creature that's been in the news.

What is this strange beast you keep hearing about?

Together, I think we can figure it out. . . .

The beasty is called an American Trump.

Its skin is bright orange, its figure is plump;

Its fur so complex, you might get enveloped.

Its hands are, sadly, underdeveloped.

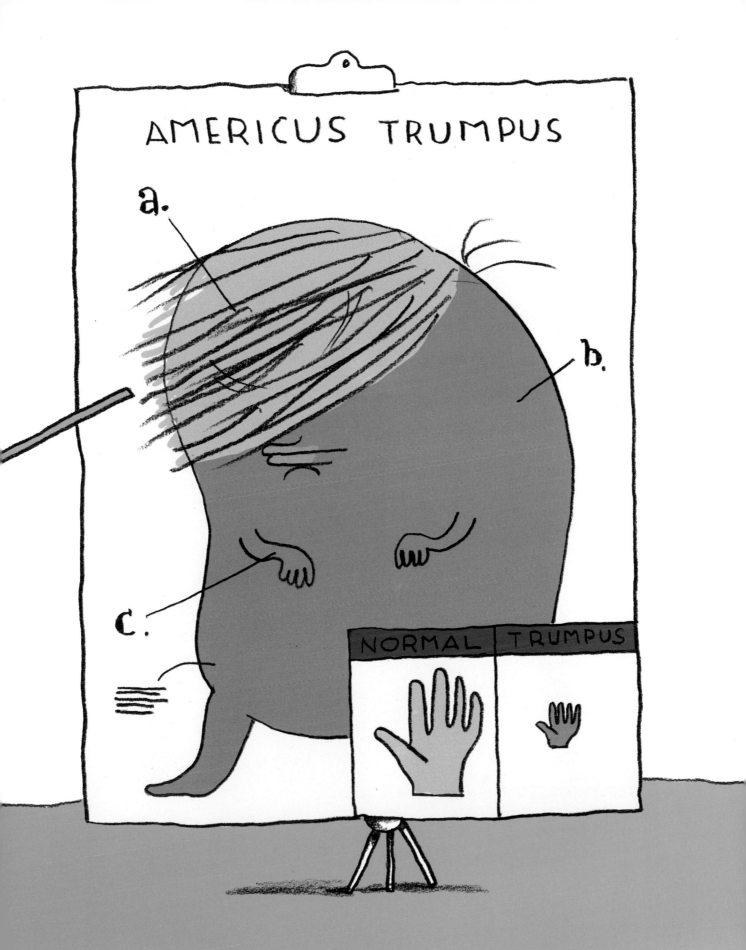

Now, where does it live? On flat-screen TVs!
It rushes toward every camera it sees.
It thrives in the most contentious conditions
And excretes the most appalling emissions.

Its diet is cash, its friends all go-getters.
Its poop spells out "Trump" in ten-foot-high letters!

Trump this and Trump that, and Trump buildings and steaks.
Trump airplanes and clothing and several Trump mates.
Trump crap everywhere in a Trumpy Trump land.
But don't call it crap. The Trump calls it a "brand."

Yes, it can speak! Are you impressed?

You should be, because a Trump's really the best!

It says so if asked, and even if not.

"I'm the best!" it declares in terms overwrought.

"I have all the best words and all the best things!
My water is bottled from all the best springs!
My wine is the best, and so is my brain.
You wanna know why? Too bad! I'll explain."

(Here's where a Trump will go on at some length
On the size of its manhood and physical strength.)

When finally done with its speech, it will grin
And say, "Now I hope that you're ready to WIN!"
For winning is what a Trump loves to do best.
"We'll be winning so much, you might get depressed!"

"I've won each and every game that I've played.

Won every opinion I've ever conveyed.

Won every debate, no matter the topic.

I once had a tie—I felt philanthropic."

Making a deal? It has no superior!
Building a wall? The rest are inferior.
"My wall will be numero uno primero.
I'll pay for it using another's dinero."

And there is the crux of the Americus Trumpus:
The swagger, the boasting, the oversized rump-us.

Its bluster's exceeded by total flamboyance.
It even makes claims of having clairvoyance:
"I KNEW this would happen!" it says aplenty.
Its hindsight is clocked at twenty and twenty.

T-RUMP

So what should you do with a Trump running wild?
The answer is all up to you, my dear child.
Run away screaming? Or maybe you fight it?
Reason and logic will only incite it.

You can cover your ears or run up a tree,
But the best thing to do is . . .

. . . turn off your TV.

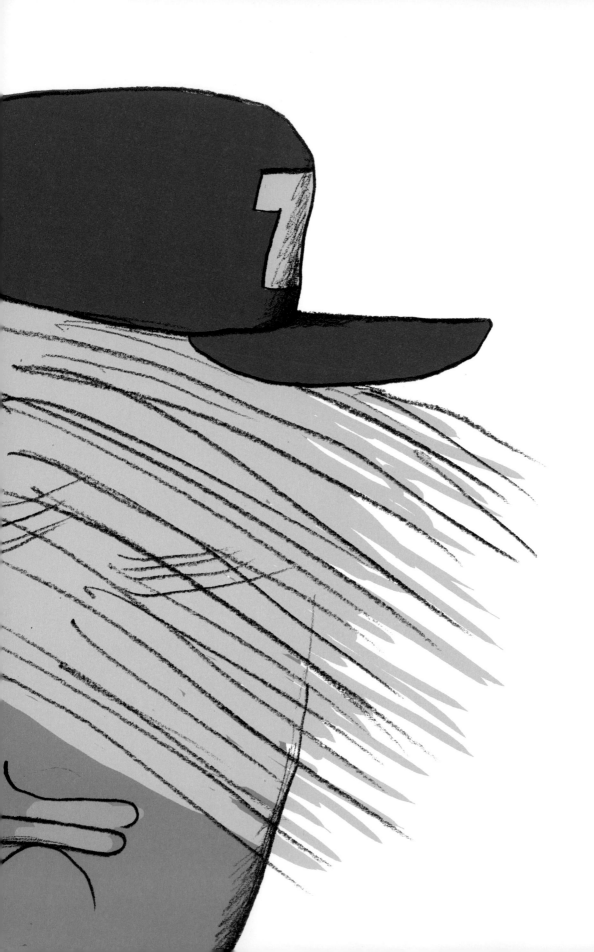

For all of the Trump's astounding uniqueness,
It certainly has a curious weakness:
A Trump loves to dine on hatred and violence;
It cannot endure a moment of silence.

It's true! A Trump needs all of our noise to exist.

Without chaos, it shrinks to a sad, orange disc.

So, should you stumble upon one in the wood,

I'm not sure what you'll do; I know what you should:

Don't respond to its brags, its taunts, or its jeers;
Ignoring a Trump is a Trump's biggest fear.

But if that plan fails and it keeps coming forth,
I hear there's an absence of Trumps in the North.